Animals on the M

Contents

What is migration?

Migration is a long journey that some animals make from one place to another, usually at the same time every year. Migrating animals follow a route they know to reach another place.

Animals migrate in the way that's safest for them. Most travel in big groups, but some migrate alone. Being in a big group can provide protection, but not always. Tiny birds, like hummingbirds, migrate alone because it's harder for their enemies to spot them separately.

Ruby-throated hummingbirds migrate 800 kilometres over the sea, all by themselves.

Every winter, Emperor penguins march across Antarctica in large groups to feed their chicks.

Some animals use the position of the sun and moon in the sky to help them find their way. Scientists think some migrating animals have a built-in **compass** to stop them from getting lost.

The Wandering albatross flies huge distances, but always finds its way home again.

Why do animals migrate?

Animals migrate to survive. They may need to travel to find food and water. There might not be enough to eat because food has run out, or because a change in the weather has made food hard to find. They have to move on, or starve to death.

Norway lemmings migrate when there are so many of them that there's not enough food for them all to eat.

Many animals migrate to have babies. They travel to a place where the weather is warmer, to give their babies the best chance of survival. When the babies are big and strong enough, they can migrate back to cooler climates.

Turtles lay their eggs on **tropical** beaches. The eggs are buried in the sand and kept warm by the hot sun.

At sea

The oceans are full of migrating animals. Many are travelling in search of food. When summer arrives in the **Arctic**, the ice melts in some places. This makes it easier to hunt for food. Some sea creatures migrate to the Arctic in summer, because there's so much to eat there.

During summer, walruses hunt for shellfish in the Arctic.

When winter comes, many sea animals swim to warm waters to have babies. They may ride on **ocean currents** to help them cover long distances. Some sea animals, for example seals, migrate back to cooler waters with their babies. Others, such as turtles, leave their babies to find their own way.

a Northern fur seal and her pup near the coast of California, USA

Humpback whale

Humpback whales migrate further than any other mammal. Every year, they swim from **polar** waters to tropical seas and then back again. Humpbacks live for up to 50 years, swimming hundreds of thousands of kilometres in a lifetime.

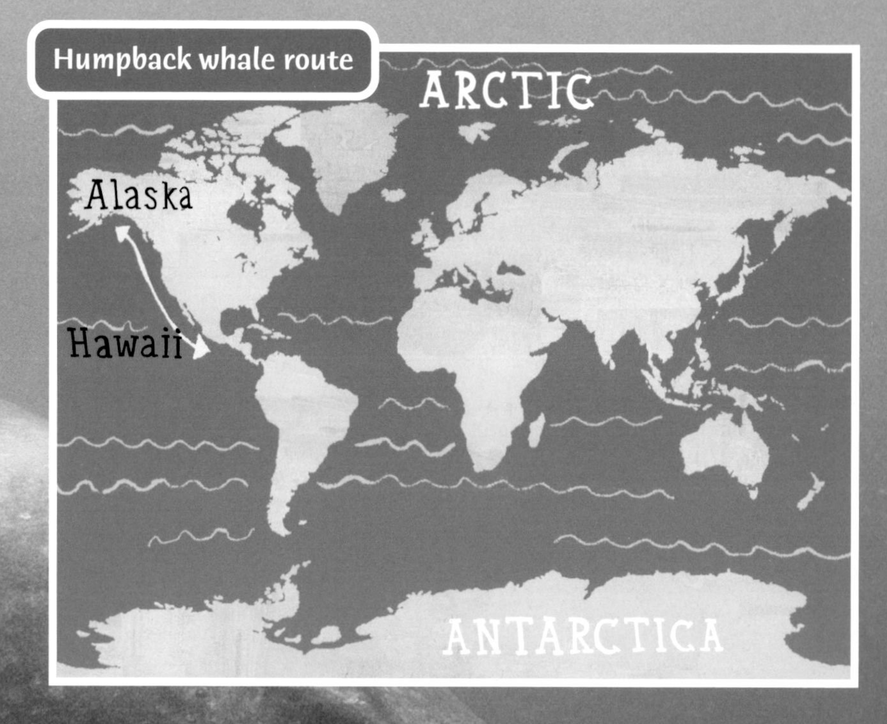

female Humpback whale and calf

Some Humpback whales spend the summer in the Arctic, where there is plenty of food to eat. As winter begins, they swim south to warmer waters, where they **breed**. The journey takes about 40 days. During this time, they don't eat anything, but live off the fat they put on during the summer.

Every year, Humpback whales travel from Alaska to Hawaii, then back again. This is about 16,900 kilometres.

Pacific salmon

Pacific salmon hatch in the rivers of Asia and North America, then migrate to the North Pacific Ocean, where there's lots of food to eat. Years later, in summer, they travel back to the rivers where they were born, to lay their eggs. Then they die, leaving their babies to start the whole journey again.

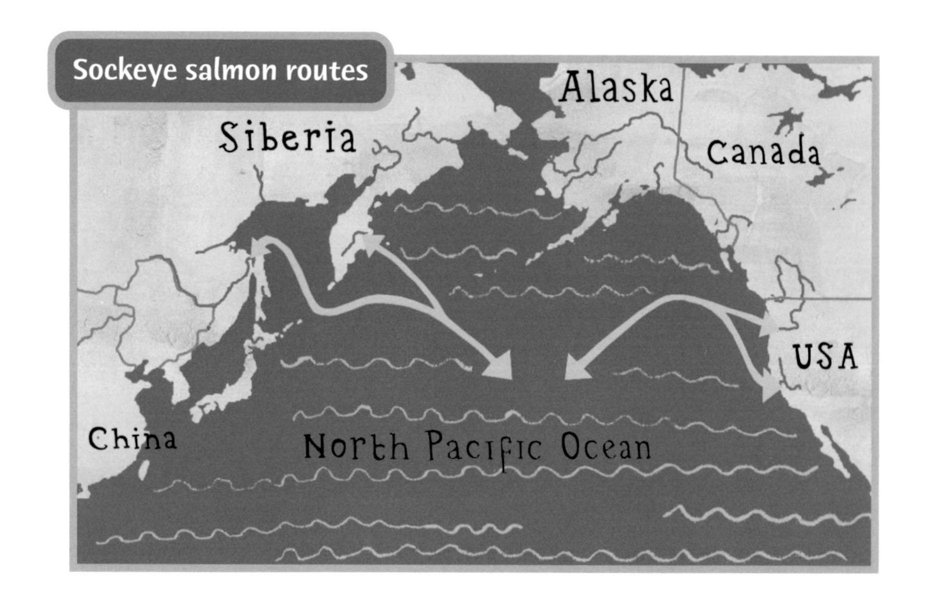

There are nine different kinds of Pacific salmon, of which one is the Sockeye salmon. Some salmon can live up to six years and will travel tens of thousands of kilometres in a lifetime.

Pacific salmon hatch and die in the same place.

Salmon can remember the smell of the river where they hatched, so as to find exactly the right place to breed. They swim against the current to travel up rivers. Sometimes they even have to leap up waterfalls.

Pacific salmon leaping up a waterfall in Alaska

Leatherback turtle

Leatherback turtles spend the winter in cool, northern waters, where they can eat jellyfish, the food they like best. In spring, they migrate to warmer waters in the south to have their babies. One group of Leatherbacks travels all the way from Canada's Atlantic coast to the Caribbean Sea.

Leatherback turtle route

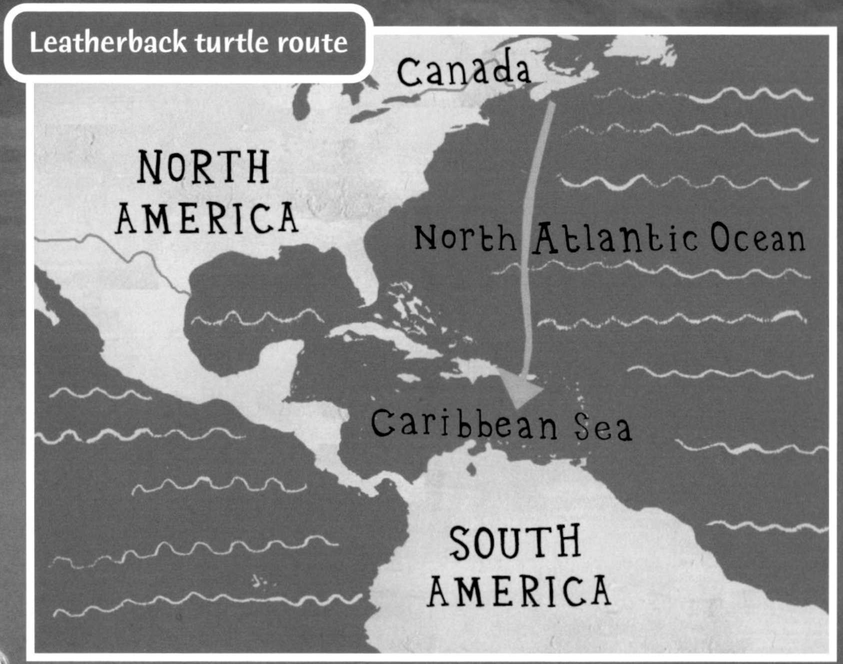

Leatherback turtles dive deeper than any other kind of turtle – over a kilometre below the waves!

After swimming south for 9,600 kilometres, a female Leatherback turtle crawls on to a warm beach to lay her eggs. Between March and July, she lays six **clutches** of eggs. When the summer is over, she swims back north again, leaving her babies to look after themselves.

In the air

Birds fly huge distances very quickly when they migrate. Some birds fly together in a V-shaped flock. Air flows smoothly behind the leader, making it easier for the rest of the flock to keep up. Migrating birds find their way by using the sun, moon and stars.

migrating Snow geese

Birds are not the only flying creatures that migrate. In spring, flocks of female Mexican free-tailed bats fly from Mexico to south-western America, where they gather in caves to have babies. No one knows why they fly so far from home to give birth. When winter begins, the bats fly back south.

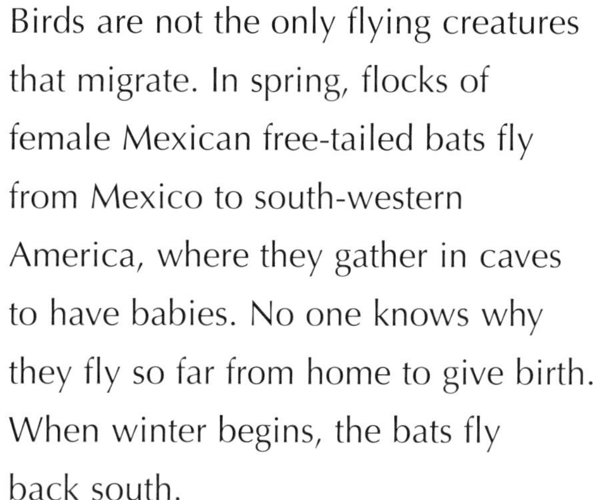

Mexican free-tailed bats flying north for the summer

a flock of Monarch butterflies roosting on a tree

Every autumn, Monarch butterflies fly from North America to Mexico, to escape the cool winter. This journey takes two months. The butterflies go back north in the spring.

Arctic tern

Arctic terns live in Antarctica between November and March, when it's summer there and not too cold. As winter starts, Arctic terns migrate north. When they arrive in the Arctic, summer is just beginning. Every year, Arctic terns enjoy two long summers. The summer sun doesn't set in the Arctic and Antarctica, so Arctic terns live most of their lives in constant daylight.

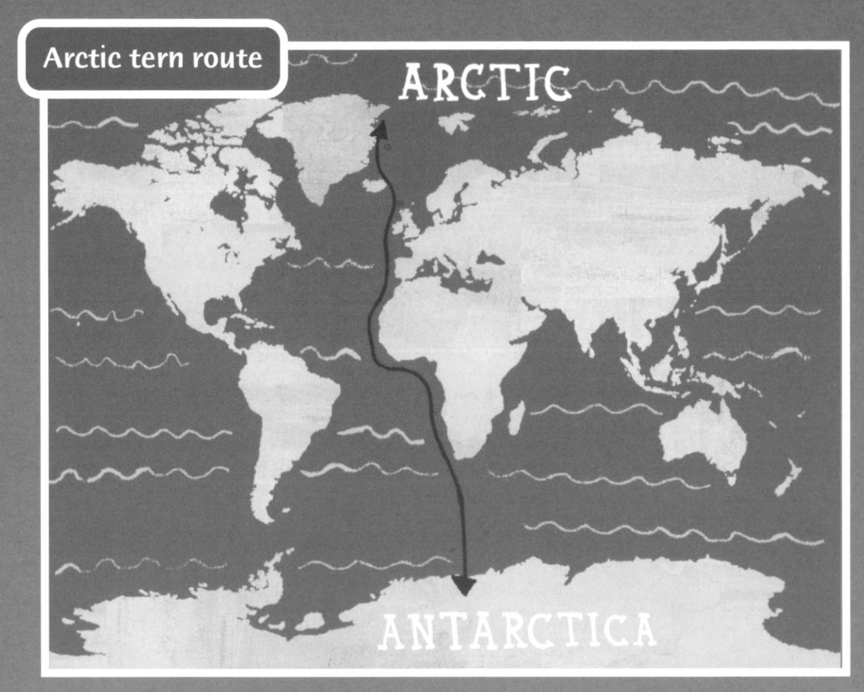

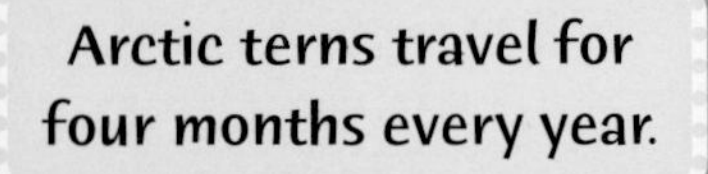
Arctic terns travel for four months every year.

Arctic terns migrate further than any other living creature. Every year, they fly 40,000 kilometres. Arctic terns start migrating when they're about three years old and live for up to 30 years. In a lifetime, they fly as far as the moon and back!

Baby Arctic terns migrate with their parents.

Swallow

In summer, British swallows build nests and have their babies in the United Kingdom. In autumn, they fly south to miss the winter cold. They travel by day, flying low to catch insects and scoop up water. Swallows take about ten weeks to reach South Africa, where they stay for about three months every year.

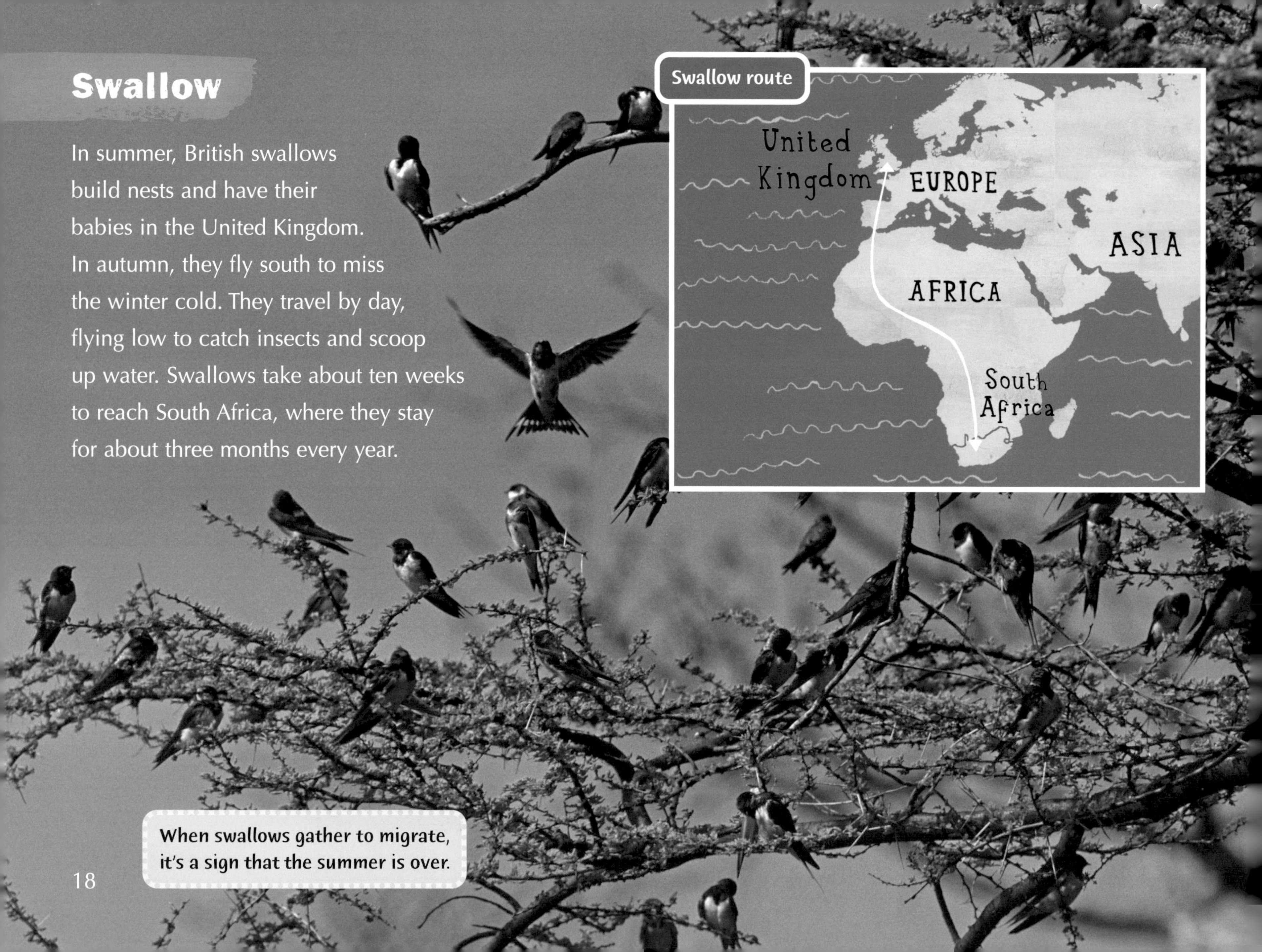

When swallows gather to migrate, it's a sign that the summer is over.

Migrating swallows fly up to 300 kilometres a day, at speeds of about 35 kilometres per hour. The total distance they fly every year is about 10,000 kilometres. Many swallows die from starvation, or are killed in storms along the way. Like many birds, some swallows are **tagged** with electronic tagging equipment so that scientists can learn more about how they migrate.

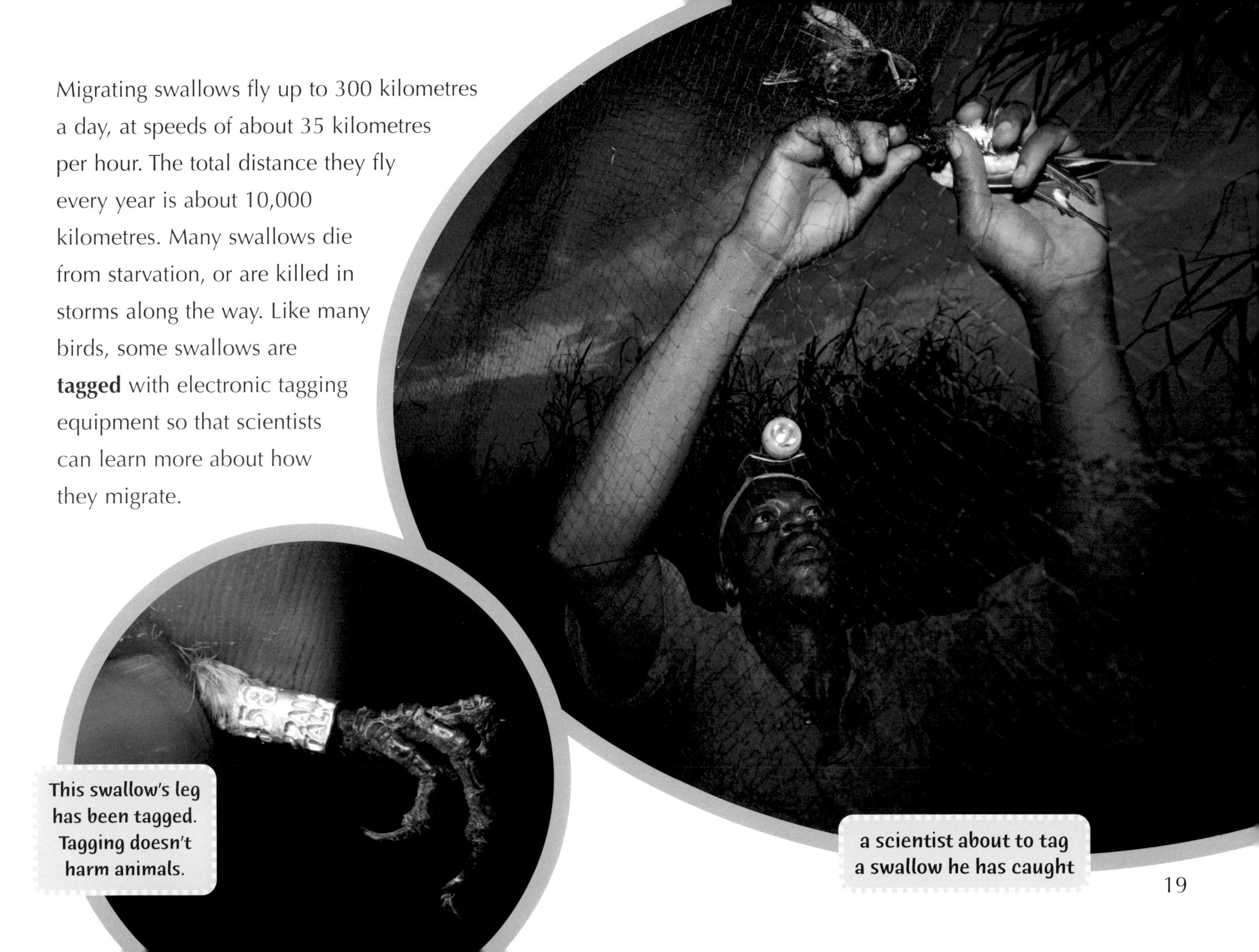

This swallow's leg has been tagged. Tagging doesn't harm animals.

a scientist about to tag a swallow he has caught

On land

Animals that migrate on land often have to cross difficult landscapes, such as mountains or even volcanoes. They can't rely on water or air currents to help them, like animals that swim or fly. For this reason, land migrations are usually shorter than those in the sea or sky.

Galapagos land iguanas climb a rocky volcano to lay their eggs at the top.

Migrating land animals often use their senses of sight or smell to help them find the way. Scientists track the journeys of some land animals as well, to find out how far and how fast they travel.

a scientist putting a tagging collar on an elephant

In eastern Africa, about two million animals go wherever the rain falls in order to find food and water. They travel all the time around the grassy plains of the Serengeti. Wildebeest, gazelles and zebras all join in this famous migration.

The Serengeti migration is the world's biggest movement of animals.

Caribou

Reindeer live in Arctic lands, such as Lapland, Siberia and Alaska. In North America, reindeer are called caribou. During summer, caribou graze on flat, Arctic plains. In winter, snow covers the ground, so the caribou have nothing to eat. Huge, hungry herds migrate south to warmer parts of Alaska and Canada, where there's food. When the snow melts in spring, they return home to breed.

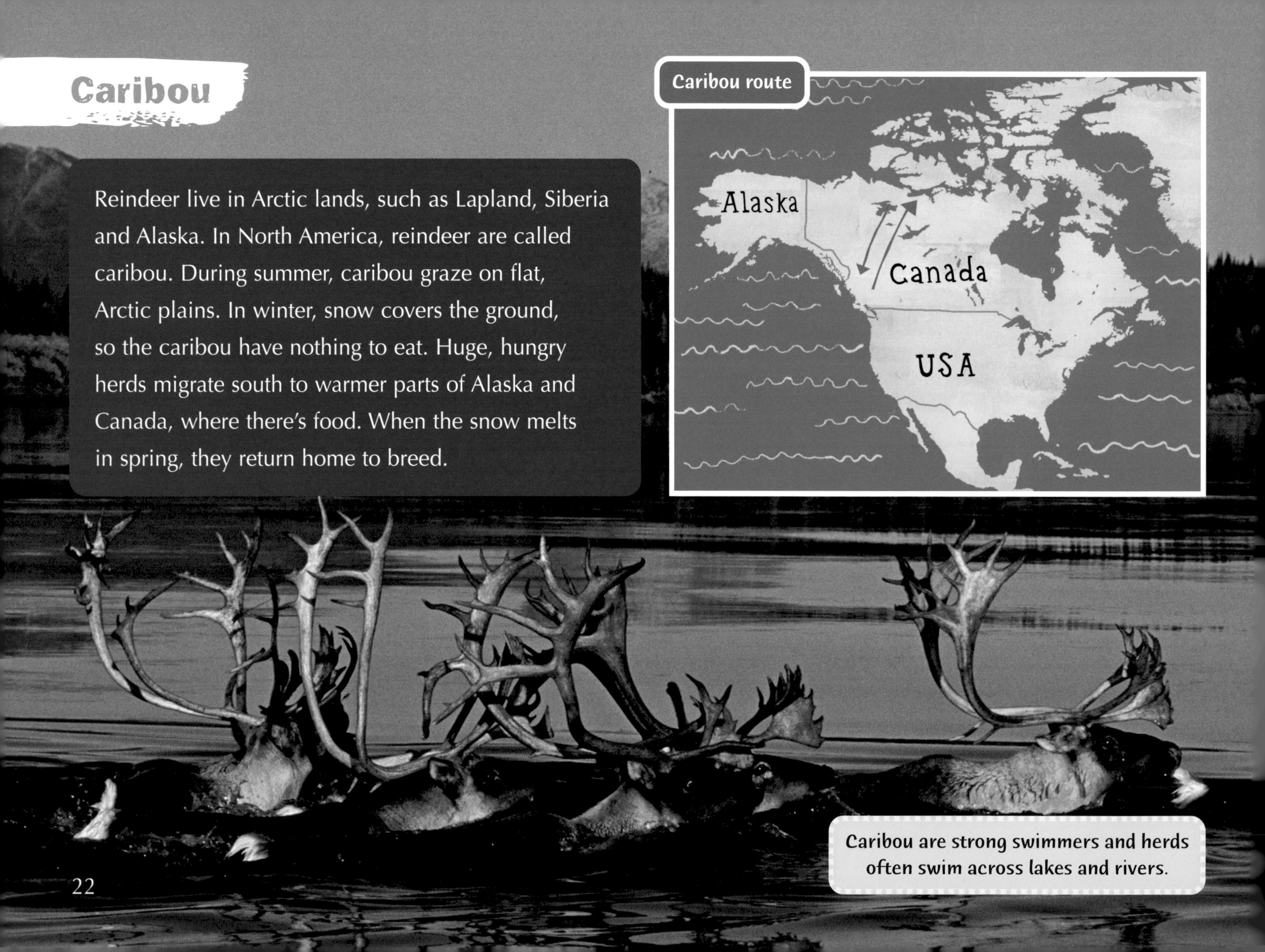

Caribou are strong swimmers and herds often swim across lakes and rivers.

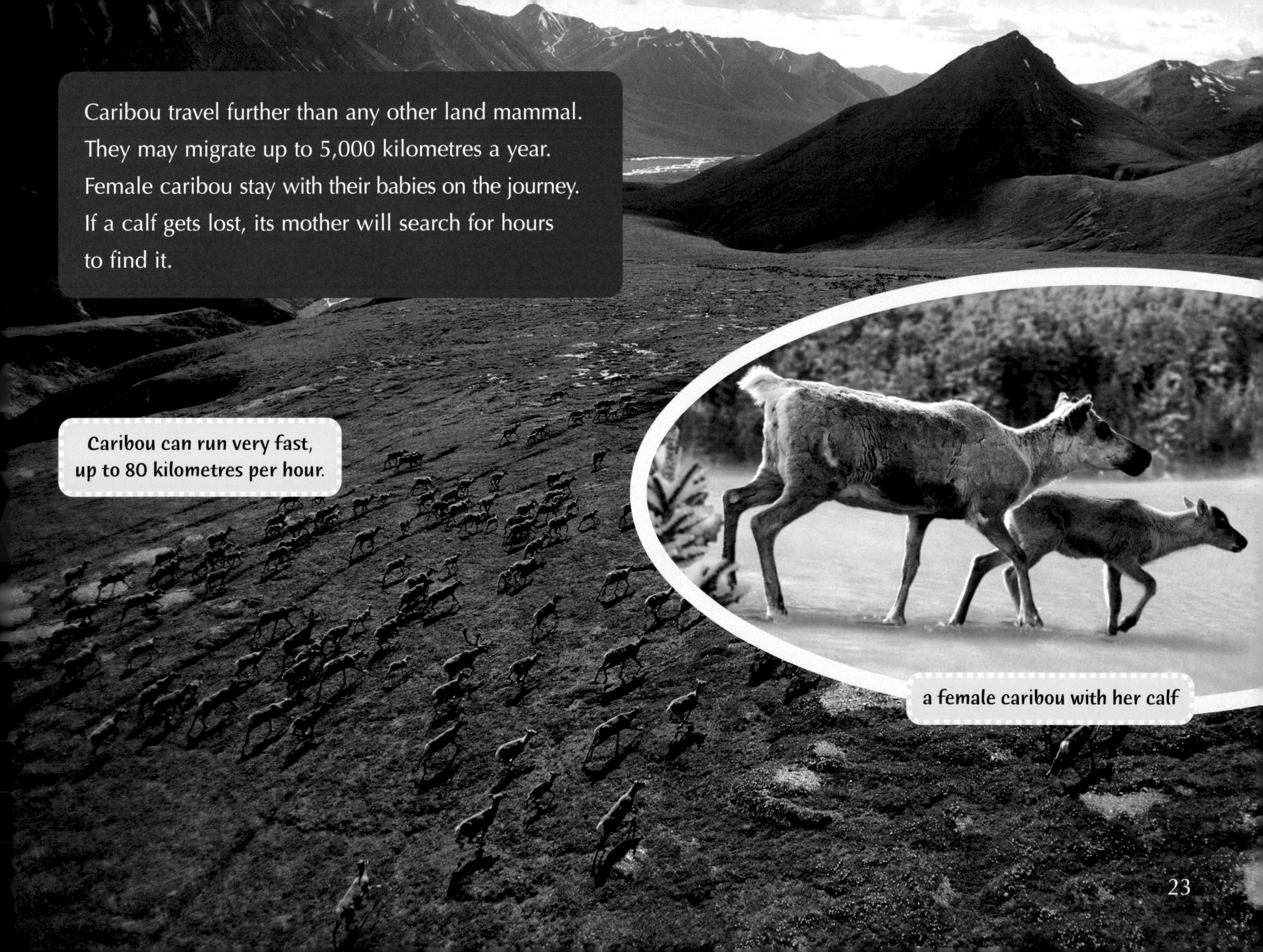

Caribou travel further than any other land mammal. They may migrate up to 5,000 kilometres a year. Female caribou stay with their babies on the journey. If a calf gets lost, its mother will search for hours to find it.

Caribou can run very fast, up to 80 kilometres per hour.

a female caribou with her calf

African elephant

Baby elephants grow up in herds of about ten family members. Elephant herds are led by an adult female. They're always on the move, looking for food and water. Between April and October, the world's largest elephant migration happens in Botswana. About 45,000 elephants travel up to 300 kilometres to find water, ending up at the Chobe River.

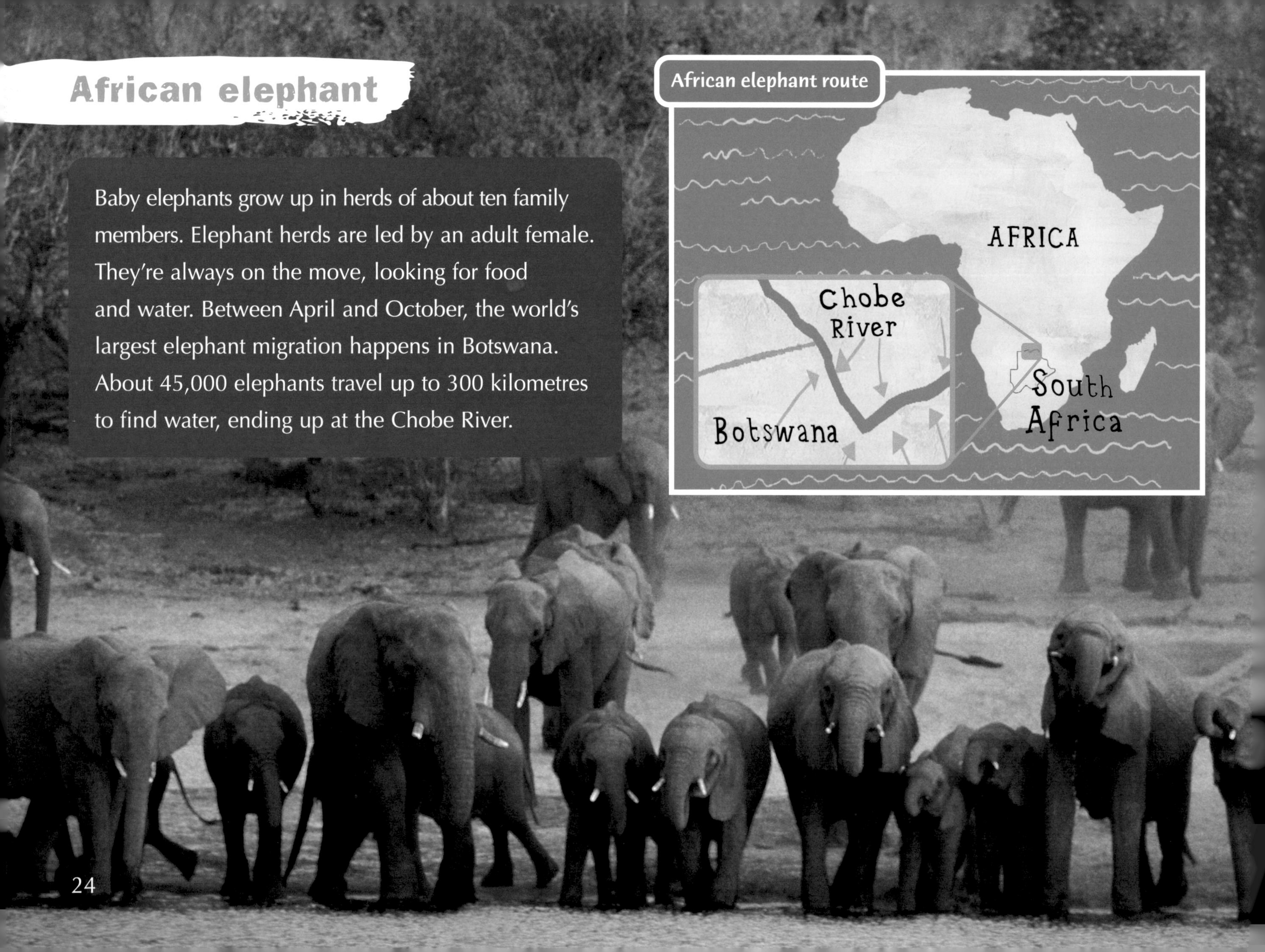

Adult male elephants live apart from family herds and migrate in a different way from adult females. Every year, when it's time for a male elephant to breed, he migrates to find a mate. He travels alone for up to three months, covering hundreds of kilometres.

a male African elephant migrating to find a mate

Changing habitats

When animals migrate, they rely on good feeding, resting and breeding places. If just one of these places is damaged or destroyed, the animals can't finish their journey. Natural **habitats** must be protected, so that migration can continue.

This turtle nesting site has become a tourist beach.

In Africa, when elephants try to follow old migration routes through grassland or forest, they often find roads, fields or villages in their way. This brings them close to people, which puts them in danger. Large areas of land can be turned into **wildlife reserves** to protect animals on the move.

This African wildlife reserve keeps migrating animals safe.

Glossary

Antarctica	the frozen continent around the South Pole
Arctic	the area around the North Pole
breed	to have babies
clutches	sets of eggs in a nest
compass	an instrument used for finding directions which has a magnetised needle
habitats	environments where animals live
ocean currents	streams of water that move through oceans
polar	near the North or South Pole
tagged	using special equipment to follow an animal's movements
tropical	a very hot and humid part of the world
wildlife reserves	protected areas of natural habitats

Index

Migration routes

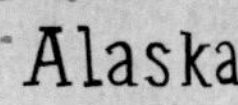

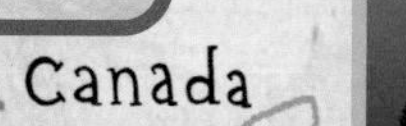

Alaska

Canada

United Kingdom

EUROPE

NORTH AMERICA

USA

North Atlantic Ocean

SOUTH AMERICA

- Humpback whale route
- Sockeye salmon routes
- Leatherback turtle route
- Arctic tern route
- Swallow route
- Caribou route
- African elephant route